T0194335

POEMS
with a Purpose

Rhyming Verse That Speaks to the Soul

REV. PAUL E. YANKE

WESTBOW
PRESS®
A DIVISION OF THOMAS NELSON
& ZONDERVAN

Scriptures taken from the Holy Bible, New International Reader's Version®, NIrV® Copyright © 1995, 1996, 1998, 2014 by Biblica, Inc.™ Used by permission of Zondervan. www.zondervan.com The "NIrV" and "New International Reader's Version" are trademarks registered in the United States Patent and Trademark Office by Biblica, Inc.™

WestBow Press books may be ordered through booksellers or by contacting:

WestBow Press
A Division of Thomas Nelson & Zondervan
1663 Liberty Drive
Bloomington, IN 47403
www.westbowpress.com
1 (866) 928-1240

ISBN: 978-1-9736-6341-6 (sc)
ISBN: 978-1-9736-6340-9 (e)

Print information available on the last page.

WestBow Press rev. date: 05/30/2019

Dedicated to my loving Christian Parents;
Eno and Grace Yanke

Contents

A Christian Christmas Eve

It was the Eve before Christmas and all through the church,
the pastor was wondering about God's people in verse.

Had they opened their Bible, even once during the Advent Season,
so that God through the Holy Spirit might with their hearts reason.

Had they read the Christmas Story, taken five minutes to even take a look?
To see what treasures God has preserved for us in His Great Holy Book.

Would people of faith continue to follow all of God's Word and not remain aloof,
see for over 2000 years it's been the standard for Christian families, it's the truth!

Will they let the devil Internet cause their hearts after this world to lust,
by just letting their Bible set on the shelf or the coffee table to collect dust.

Had they through prayer cleared their minds for the service that evening,
so that what God had to offer them to their souls would be pleasing.

Young parents can't you see that worshiping on just Christmas and Easter,
isn't enough because the devil attacks your children constantly and never makes life easier.

Because of the love God the Father has shown us in sending His only Son,
our plight through faith to relieve,
we especially during this season should be open to the hearts of other's
needs, and truly their hurting perceive.

Perhaps during the last year a friend or loved one God has called home to
heaven their mate,
so let the love of Christ show through us to relieve loneliness and despair,
it's never too late!

Can you bake cookies, if not maybe you can sing?
Go visit some shut-ins and let the love of Christ ring.

In our world of messed up values even Christians forget
that St. Nicholas isn't the founder of giving of gifts,
Rather God in all His Omnipotent Glory giving His Son first,
that through faith all mankind He lifts.

Many parents allow their children to make up their schedules,
but do they realize that God needs the playing field to be level.

Without allowing time in their schedules for the preaching and teaching
of God's Holy Word,
their children are going to make decisions that I'm sorry are bad and in
reality just absurd.

Do sugarplums dance in all of their heads?
Or are they willing by the Holy Spirit to be lead.

Has the world with the devils help convinced them to think only of
themselves in this land?
Or have they been blessed to feel what it's like to be one of God's extended
hands.

Think about how Mary must have felt
when by the angel Gabriel she was approached,
and told God has chosen you to conceive His Son
through the Holy Ghost. (Luke 1:26-35)

To shepherds keeping watch over their flocks by night,
the angel appeared to them in a great heavenly light. (Luke 2:8-16)

Today in the town of David a Savior has been born to set hearts on fire,
and then praising God that angel was joined by a great heavenly choir.
(Luke 2:11)

When the angelic choir had left the shepherds hurried to Bethlehem to see,
God's Son a Holy sight, (Luke 2:15-16)
Because they realized into this world of darkness, God the Father had
brought the One and only Light. (John 1:4)

Can people appreciate the majesty of using a glorious star?
to announce Christ's birth to the Wise Men from afar. (Matthew 2:1-2)

If you want your life in this world to be lifted up high,
then allow Christ to enter your heart and your soul will fly!

So don't let the wiles of the devil into your heart shove,
because Christ Jesus your Savior, you a sinner does love!

This Christmas Season my prayer is that He reminds you that with the help
of the Holy Spirit you are His Light,
so go out with God's Sword of the Spirit and spread the good news that
more be brought from darkness into a life Bright! (Ephesians 6:17-18)

Composed by the Holy Spirit and written by Reverend Paul E. Yanke

A Father's and A Grandfather's Prayer

When a baby's on its way Lord, just let it be healthy,
Girl or boy it doesn't matter either one will be stealthy,
give me strength to raise it as a Christian and I'll be wealthy.
Psalm 86:1-6, Proverbs 8:15, 29

Hold that baby in your arms and you will see with ease,
its tiny hands and feet patterned in God's image to please.
Genesis 1:27

My grandfather said, "You are a child and you are to be seen, and not heard."
If only children today would honor their father and mother and be corrected with just one word.
Exodus 20:12

As the child begins to grow and a non-God pleasing attitude begins to show,
a loving father the line must tow, and Biblical correction may be the only way to go.
Proverbs 13:24

Paul states in Ephesians Chapter six, verse four, fathers your children do not exasperate,

instead bring them up in the training and instruction of the Lord on this elaborate.
Ephesians 6:4

Pray often for the welfare of your children, and on your knees with the Lord collaborate,
when you knock God answers with His Word and the Holy Spirit your child's heart saturates.
Matthew 7:7-11

God gave children parents so that lovingly we can share our life's sour grapes,
may our branches heed the wisdom, make corrections, and be spared the same mistakes.
Proverbs 15:5

But, mistakes are children must make some on their own, it's part of God's plan,
guidance we are to give because they are on loan, so wiser be then when they began.
Proverbs 14:26, 27

God likes us to have fun with our kids, but be careful with being their buddy,
because if that's all you are with them, when discipline is called for things get muddy.

Please help me model Christian behavior, so dissention I do not fuel,
or surely model me in public they will, making me the fool!
Exodus 20, Matthew 22:37-40

Teach your children the Ten Commandments, their wisdom taught should become your home rule,
and when kids brave the world as a guide they'll have a top notch tool.
Proverbs 30:5, Romans 6:23

I may not have the money of the man down the street, or the neighbor's successful business with a large truck fleet.

Don't let me fail before you I in heaven meet, to be my kids faithful Christian dad is the greatest feat.

God answers prayer I know it 'tis true, because hair raising moments I've had a few,
in spite of my fatherhood sometimes sinfully askew, you've made our children Christians born anew.
Matthew 21:22, Mark 11:24, John 3:3

Please Lord craft me into a better grandfather than a father I pray by the tons,
since it would be a shame to waste all the wisdom gained by three trial runs!

Composed by the Holy Spirit and written by Reverend Paul E. Yanke

A Father's Prayer

I pray for men, who are determined to succeed in this important responsibility,
how much our world needs fathers who committed to their families will be.
1 Timothy 3:4,5

A foolish son is his fathers ruin, brings grief, piles up sadness in a heap,
honor your father and mother, keep this commandment and your heart
with gladness will leap.
Proverbs 19:13,25, Matthew 15:4, Exodus 20:12, Mark 7:10, Deuteronomy
5:16

A father must manage his own family well,
that with respect his children will swell.
1 Timothy 3:4

Listen to your human father, who gave you earthly life,
and don't despise your mother when she ages a trife.
Proverbs 23:22

As a father, train up a child in the way he should go and he will not depart,
God promises with instruction he will steadfast remain and through Jesus
heaven will impart.
Proverbs 22:6, Ephesians 6:4

God is a father in the perfect sense; he's what every father should try to be,
he disciplines; he cares; he guides; he loves; his son Jesus set us free.
John 3:16

If only men would realize we are to mirror God the Father as head of our family,
how much clearer a child's image of the heavenly father in their life, would be.
Ephesians 5:1, 6:4

A Christian father prays for his children every day,
that the devil against them will have no sway.
2 Timothy 2:3

That their daily sins with contrition on Jesus they will lay,
so they continue to pray, walk and grow in the Biblical way.
Romans 6

It would be hard to be a good father, if no guide had ever been written,
God the father is our example, take a look at the Bible and you will be smitten.
Matthew 7:11, John 20:31

My prayer for all of mankind in this big messed up world of sin,
turn the hearts of fathers to their children and children to their kin.
Malachi 4:6

Children I implore you no matter what your earthly father is like,
you can run to your father in heaven, whether adult, teen, or tike.
1 Peter 5:7, Psalm 55:22

If God were your Father, you would love me,
like Father; like Son, I (Jesus) will you see.
John 8:42

Composed by the Holy Spirit and written by Reverend Paul E. Yanke
For Father's Day

A Grandmother's Prayer

The world is in trouble, it's coming apart at the seams this is plain to see,
if others would only open their eyes and ears in thought they would be
with me.

My grandmother had a stubborn endurance that was educational and
endearing to me,
five major surgeries, three strokes that crippled and yet uncomplaining
was she.

She got her speech back and with practice the use of her hand,
her faith an inspiration to all and on it an army could stand. Matthew 16:18

A true story my grandmother told; was beans for all three meals a day,
because she grew up during the Great Depression,
she enjoyed so much the satisfaction of hard work, and every day was a
chance to teach with sincere expression.

She taught us by example to pray before meals and at bedtime as well,
to be honest with God, confess our sins sincerely and the truth to Him tell.
(Sermon on the Mount) Matthew chapters 5-7

Not much for material possessions in this world, she considered herself
rich in her families love,
God blessed her and grandpa with many years together and blessings from
above. Deuteronomy 6:1,2

Pray for all your children, grandchildren, and greats, teach them to be successful instilling all they need to know.
Done when children are young, the Bible states; even when they are old they'll know which way to go. Proverbs 22:6

Maybe just maybe think about it, your own grandmother; was very similar to mine,
living her life as a sinner, as best she could; according to God's Almighty design. Psalm 51:5

When I close my eyes I can see her plainly enjoying life, sitting in her favorite chair,
always designing projects, knitting, crocheting, and sewing gifts, with us her kids to share.

Her Bible was never far away from her, to be read keeping her faith strong, now she's living in a perfect mansion, with Jesus in heaven where her spirit does belong. Matthew 24:42-44

Composed by the Holy Spirit and written by Reverend Paul E. Yanke

A Hunter's Prayer - The Biblical Perspective

The first thing I need to say is that God is Omniscient it is true,
which means He knows all about His creation what man would say and do.

God placed Adam and Eve in the garden as caretakers, you may eat whatever you can harvest, but one act is forbidden,
thou shalt not eat of the tree of the knowledge of good and evil, but man sinned; felt ashamed and thought from God they were hidden.

Then the man and his wife heard the sound of the Lord God walking in the garden in the cool of the day,
The Lord God called to man; "Where are you?" I was naked man did say.
God responded "you've sinned," now you must pay. (Genesis 3:10.11)

God asked "Who told you that you were naked?" Have you eaten from the tree that I commanded you not to eat?, (Genesis 3:10-11)
because of the nakedness of sin, and no cloth at the time, God Himself slew the first animal to cover man from head to feet!

God stated; "I will not kill you" as I had promised for this sin against My Will, (Genesis 2:17)
but now no longer will life be easy because to eat the land you must till. (Genesis 3:17)

Another major change was made concerning mankind's diet, how they would subsist and what to eat,
man not only would till the soil, but could head to the woods to hunt in search of meat.

Genesis Twenty-Five records the story of Isaac and Rebekah's sons, Jacob, a quiet man and Esau, a mighty hunter,
while Jacob's choice was to tend the flocks, Isaac loved wild game, and Esau went out to hunt in the frontier.

I think I can relate to how Esau felt when in search of game he headed to the bush,
grab my .22 rifle, chores done and head to the woods, a prayer for safety and for success I'd wish.

I was taught from young that all we have belongs to God, wild critters are no exception, so Far Chase is the rule,
prepare yourself mentally for the hunt, equipment in good shape, your weapon sighted in, nothing works better than a sharp tool.

Growing up on the farm I was taught what God provides you do not waste so when I shot squirrels, I cleaned them, they were cooked, I developed quite a taste.

As I got older, more large and diverse became the pursued wild game,
The principles didn't change, to be called a Good Sportsman that's my title name.

Remember safety first is the rule, the only right way,
every hunt is successful where you live, to hunt another day.

If you hunt only to have a trophy mount to hang upon your wall,
I don't think much of you as a sportsman you are very small, not tall.

God made wild animals especially prolific in their ability to reproduce,
thus sportsman and women are needed there excess numbers to reduce.

Those who think we should not own weapons, shoot or hunt their ideas they must prune,
see deer starve to death or hit one with their vehicle and they'll soon change their tune.

When you're out in the woods, some call it the bush, put your senses into action take in what you smell, hear, and see,
and then tell me all this happened, fell into complete unison, insist it was an accident, common sense says it can't be.

Every time I'm in the woods I feel God's presence, and say to myself "we must preserve this hunting right,"
or future generations will never be able to experience the outdoors, the beauty of God's Creation, for mankind His insight.

I pray we will become better Sportsmen and caretakers of God's Creation we will stay,
or our God given right to hunt, trap and fish will one day decay away.

Composed by the Holy Spirit and written by Reverend Paul E. Yanke

A Mother's Prayer

Much better to not make yourself the star of the day,
the Bible says it's best to go into your closet to pray.
Matthew 6:5,6

The Priests and the Levites stood to bless the people on the first Passover in two hundred years;
Hezekiah ordered a prayer. It reached God in heaven, God heard it with his holy ears.
2 Chronicles 30:27

Therefore let everyone who is Godly pray to you, while you may certainly be found,
blessed is he who penitently prays for forgiveness, God will grant it His Word is sound.
Psalm 32:2&6

When I kept silent my bones wasted away,
through my groaning both night and day.
Psalm 3:3,4

Then you will call upon Me, and pray with all that's in you to Me,
because you seek Me with all your heart, I will listen and you will see.
Jeremiah 29:12

Often children don't honor their mother, as is God's fourth command,
but a mother will pray for children that mistreat her, no matter the demand.
Exodus 20:12, Luke 6:28

When you forgive others when they sin against you, by what they do and say,
the Father in Heaven will also forgive you your sins, for it is his way.
Matthew 6:14

Have you ever read John 10:11-13 and substituted human children in place
of the sheep, you should?
Realize that children raised in daycares by hired hands will seldom be loved
by their parents, as they could.

Mothers pray their children survive grade school, illness, next puberty,
and high school that young adults they may be.

That Sunday School lessons, Bible stories, and God's morals might stick,
so that in strong young Christians we will see a burning wick.
Proverbs 22:6

Mother's pray that each of their children will secure a spouse that with
them will highly rate,
when in reality the bible says, pray that each one finds a Christian, high
morals, life-long mate.
Genesis 2:20-24

God gave mothers wisdom to speak and manors impart,
through mother's eyes a child sees Christ's loving heart.
Proverbs 31:26

Her children arise and call her blessed, mom you surpass them all,
as mother you prayed with us and stayed with us, answered God's call.
Proverbs 31:28&29

A mother sighs, and sometimes over her children's actions she cries,
a mother prays, her children know for them Christ did arise!
Matthew, Mark, Luke, John, 1 Corinthians 15

Composed by the Holy Spirit and written by Reverend Paul E. Yanke
For Mother's Day

A Pastor's Heart

A well spoken message stirs a heart to rejoice
there is nothing like a strong, resilient voice
and when sorrow comes, there is no better gift to impart
then the gift of a caring, pastor's heart

A loving touch or a kind word
a moment of counsel from God's holy word
a telephone call or visit to mend
is the gift of our pastor's heart.

Lord, bless our pastor
on his birthday
bless his ministry along the way
for fame and fortune can never impart
the precious gift of a caring pastor's heart

Just a servant of Christ
using his gifts to tend
with a desire to love God
to the very end
tending his flock in the Savior's way
is the gift of a pastor's heart.

Striving to live
as an apostle of Christ

serving his father giving Godly advice!
preaching and teaching and sharing the Word
is the gift of a caring pastor's heart.

Composed by the Holy Spirit and written by Reverend Paul E. Yanke

An Old Fashioned Christmas

I'm dreaming of an Old Fashioned Christmas in my mind,
a time with memories that were much more kind.

Some remember Christmases when life was less hustle,
life was more simple, and hard work the bustle.

Where you received in a stocking an orange and hard candy,
one set of Sunday best, and life was just dandy.

At first the only toys were all made of wood,
but for quality and durability they sure were good.

Wrapping paper was trimmed as not to be wasted,
ironed and stored for next Christmas use, repasted.

At least two feet deep is the holiday snow,
a challenge for the horses and sleigh as they go.

One child's wish for a hand sled to take on a hill,
if it's been a good financial year we will sure have a thrill.

We remember gifts, Barbie's, trucks, and clothes,
Lincoln Logs, Easy Bake Oven, oh what a repose.

Our first Christmas tree was an evergreen,
and handmade the ornaments, oh what a scene.

Memories of Christmas in our mind we do steep,
but the true meaning of Christmas, is much more deep.

An Old Fashioned Church Christmas can't be shaken,
for without the true Christmas Story all are forsaken.

A Christmas where Jesus is by far the best,
and second is where falls all the rest. (Deuteronomy 5:7; Exodus 20:3)

Composed by the Holy Spirit and written by Reverend Paul E. Yanke

Assured Easter Joy

Some question whether Jesus on Skull Hill that Good Friday really did die, or was He just in a trance, a comma and it was all just a lie.

John's text records for us that the Roman guard pierced Jesus side with a spear, because they thought it very strange that Jesus was already dead, actually quite queer.
John 19:34

When the centurion in charge at the crucifixion felt the earthquake and saw the darkness he thought it very odd,
the Roman became terrified which convicted his heart and he declared, "Surely He was the Son of God!"
Matthew 27:54, Mark 15:39

When the women went to the tomb on that first Easter morn, they realized He is not here,
instead they saw an angel all dressed in white, "remember what He told you," as friends He held dear.
Matthew 28:5-6, Mark 16:5-7

Just look around you in Spring at all the signs of life, new buds, plants and flowers remind us of something,
a promise made, a promise kept, the tomb is empty, He is risen just as He said, our Savior, Prophet, and King.
Matthew 28:6

What does this mean for you and me upon this special Easter day?
We recall Jesus precious words, today with me in paradise you will stay.
Luke 23:43

That's not the end of the benefits for us, forgiveness of sins we have and it's free,
Jesus accomplished this for us by His resurrection, after death on that horrible tree.
Matthew 5:17, Romans 4

So when the burdens, cares, and troubles of this world weigh you down and you think you just can't go on,
Remember Jesus died in our place out of love and pronounced the words, "it is finished," and arose with "it is won."
John 19:30, and Romans 6:4

I know that there are a lot of Jews, skeptics and naysayers that say still today, "it was just a ruse,"
but then when you get down to the truth of it, "It's all about faith," truly they loose.

The Easter story is sound based on prophesies alone fulfilled,
no other opponents can make such claims, they are stilled.
Throughout the Bible

Keep an open mind, examine the evidence and you will be convinced,
Archeologists, Historians and Theologians agree it all makes sense.

Common sense tells us that Christ's resurrection from the dead, a recorded fact must be true,
why else would the Chief priests, pay off the tomb guards to lie, except to deceive you.
Matthew 28:12-14

Luke records; Peter saw, the strips of linen were lying by themselves and the Savior was no where to be found,
John goes further; he saw the burial cloth for Jesus head folded up separately, making the resurrection even more sound.
2 Samuel 22:31, John 17:17

If this were not enough to prove any case totally for the truth, beyond a shadow of a doubt,
Jesus appeared to more than five hundred of the brothers at the same time, proving He was alive and about!
1 Corinthians 15:6

Stand up and don't let the devil so easily you deceive,
rather witness to our faith, and as a child just believe!
Matthew 18:3, Matthew 19:14

Composed by the Holy Spirit and written by Reverend Paul E. Yanke

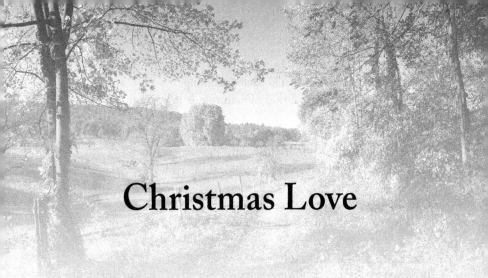

Christmas Love

Recognized Heavenly Love
So that we may understand in due time,
I give to you the story of God's love in rhyme.

It started 1400 years before His birth,
prophets foretold of a Savior that would come to earth. Deuteronomy
18:17, 18

Bethlehem is the town where Jesus was to be born,
and even though predicted by prophets, some would scorn. Micah 5:2

He was to be born in a stable manger, because no room at the inn,
born of Virgin Mary to save the world from sin. Isaiah 7:14

Men during the time of the Messiah's birth in their own sins did whorl,
because they were looking for a warrior king they missed Baby Jesus as their
pearl. Books of Jeremiah and Zephaniah

Let us recognize God's love in Jesus birth that with us it may be well,
then will the Holy Spirit through us shine so the number of believers swell.

God's Love Refines and Prepares
God's plan is so perfect and great in sending His Son
that those who are moved to faith may be won. Luke 21:28

To pave the way for the awaited Savior's coming,
God sent a messenger to bring human minds to strumming. Luke 1:13
Luke 3:1-6

Repent and be baptized John the Baptist did say,
God's Word refines and prepares you for the narrow way. Malachi 3:1-4

Christ's love is the one and only way,
with an Advent voice John did say. Luke 3:7-18

God's Love Guards and Protects
In answer to King Hezekiah's prayer Jesus appeared as "The Angel of the Lord,"
and true to Isaiah's prophesy Assyrians 185,000 slain, Sennacherib put to
the sword. 2 Kings 19:35-37

Zephaniah descendent of Hezekiah knew of this great victory,
he told the Israelites to repent in Babylonian captivity.

How we live out this day and look to the earth's end
come from our relationship with Christ, on Him we depend.

God's prophet Zephaniah some 625 years before Christ was born
helped unwrap that revelation that human hearts not be torn.

Because of Jesus, His words are comfort back then and now.
God's love guards and protects, all Christians in unison respond WOW.
Zephaniah 3:14-17

God's Love is Hope
Micah's prophecy gave the people hope for tomorrow,
It healed their depressed hearts and removed sorrow.

A baby born in Bethlehem, Thou you are small among the Judah clans,
That little one will become ruler over Israel to fulfill God's plans. Micah 5:2

He will stand and shepherd His flock in the strength of the Lord,
defend against all evil attacks by lion or bear, and the devil's evil horde.
John 10:11-14

Rule in the majesty God the Father by name,
and do His perfect best for us today just the same.

Christians will live securely for His greatness will reach earth's end,
All true believes in Jesus Christ to heaven He will send. Micah 5:2-4

Christ Love is Hope and reaches both high and low,
Through thick and thin, good and bad, salvation to sow. Luke 1:50 Old
and New Testaments

This poem is written from the lessons for the four Sundays in Advent Series
C; it reflects God's love throughout the Advent season and again delivers
the messages of the lessons listed in the poem.

Jesus and Martin Luther were both believers in using the arts to deliver the
message. I pray that God's Word is meaningful to your heart.

Composed by the Holy Spirit and written by Reverend Paul E. Yanke

Christmas Message - Another Year Ended

Well here we are again another year has come to an end,
Winter, Spring, Summer, Fall each season's needs and cares to us do lend.

When I think about the true meaning of Christmas, my thoughts go back
to previous years,
I remember only a couple of material gifts that would make me want to
stand up with cheers.

I remember my first G. I. Joe, Fort Apache, and Marx Electric Train,
the importance of these toys runs off quickly like drops of rain.

For women they may remember their first Barbie or cute baby doll with
bobbling eyes,
it's not the gift that is important, but the love and care shown by selecting
perfect buys.

As hard as you look for the meaning of Christmas, on a gaily lit evergreen
tree,
the meaning is found on another tree where Christ died, and rose on Easter
us to free.

Christmas is the season of giving; we pattern our life after Christ as a Christian must do,
but to say this earns heaven is simply not true, it erases Christ's sacrifice for me and you.

If Christ hadn't taken the place for our sins almost two thousand years ago, the ongoing relief of forgiveness as a gift to those truly penitent we wouldn't know.

When I reminisce in my mind about many Christmas Eve memories that have stuck over the years,
It's going as a family to the Candlelight Service to worship God faithfully that brings tears.

We can work up such a feeling of hopelessness, as with the help of the devil our problems we ponder,
And then all of a sudden by prayer and the power of the Holy Spirit, there is hope in the Babe and star yonder.

The Advent Wreath reminds us Advent is through and Christmas is here, please give your loved ones a hug and share Christ's good cheer.

Charles Dickens wrote "A Christmas Carol" to teach us that Christmas is a time to be generous to all mankind without exception,
If we want our children to see with eyes of God's love, then teach of Christ's birth, His death and Easter resurrection.

The Bible tells us in Christ's own words, "cast all your cares upon me," 1 Peter 5:7
then into the years to come we can sail through this world's tyranny.
Bible books referenced: Matthew, Mark, Luke, John, Psalm 51 & 55, Micah, and Isaiah
Composed by the Holy Spirit and written by Reverend Paul E. Yanke

Christmas Message In Rhyme

T'was the night before Christmas when all through the church,
the pastor was stirring with concern and in rhyming verse.

His thoughts were on the sheep that God had placed in his care,
a he knew the celebration of Christmas would soon be there.

Because of the commercialization of Christmas the pastor is concerned,
that the true meaning of Christmas CHRIST must be relearned.

Could he use items of Christmas and associate them with the Bible Holiday,
to teach the true meaning of Christmas and importance it would play.

Just like the Grinch who tried to steal Christmas found out you can't take what's in the WHO'S hearts,
The devil through his scheming, lying and cheating can't take from our souls the faith the Holy Spirit imparts. John 10:29

The evergreen tree reminds me that left to my own sinful nature I'm a dope,
but through baptism I'm a tree planted in a stream of living water that gives hope. Jeremiah 17:7&8

A candy cane made by hand and shaped like a "J",
reminds us Jesus is Christ our Savior and our stay.

Christmas Wreaths made in a continuous circle that have no end,
tells us God's love is perfect, lasting forever we need not pretend.

Candles and bulbs placed everywhere all aglow in the night,
remind us that Jesus Christ of life is the true light.

Tinsel and garland hung with care do not make the Bible Message bright,
but rather a quiet and gentle spirit is very precious in God's Sight. 1 Peter
3:3&4

The construction of the Universe reminds us of God's great unending
power,
by Christ's sacrifice, eternal life and forgiveness of sins as blessings He did
shower.
Genesis 1, Romans 5:1&2

I bring you good news of great joy for all people today,
the babe, the Messiah born in Bethlehem the devil did slay. Luke 2:1-7,
Genesis 3:15

So we make a joyful noise to the Lord, we worship the Lord with gladness,
that He worked such a plan of salvation, using Jesus His Son to end all
sadness.
Psalm 92 & 93

Christmas Day a true Biblical celebration always will be,
As long as Christ as Messiah with God's help we do see!

Composed by the Holy Spirit and written by Reverend Paul E. Yanke

Christmas - From Darkness Into Light

John 1:1- 18, Isaiah 52:7-10, Hebrews 1:1-12

Like Genesis, the Gospel of John starts before creation was made,
in the beginning was the Word, Jesus was here when foundations were laid.

The Word and God are here described as two distinct persons, God the Father and Son,
in Genesis 1:2, "The Spirit was hovering over the waters completing the Triune God, Three in one.

Jesus was the agent, by whom God spoke the entire creation into being,
like a master workman Proverbs 8:30 says, the complete project over-seeing.

God had a plan for the mankind He had made,
for a perfect relationship with man foundations were laid.

With the help of the devil, man acted on the sin that was in his mind,
now all of mankind towards the wonders of God are made blind. Genesis 3

God spoke to our fathers by the prophets, judges and kings, at many times and in many a way,

But the people continued to sin, couldn't see God's grace, or that he was with them every day.

Things haven't changed much, the world we live in is spiritually ignorant, and without sight,
If creation should be redeemed from darkness of sin and death, then God would have to make known his Son's Light!

But how would God do this? He would come to the place where we are, descend to earth,
"The Word became flesh and dwelt among us," His Son would be born in a stable, by virgin birth. John 1:14, Isaiah 7:14

All this had to take place, because man could no longer find his creator.
So do you recognize your Maker now, dear Christians? Sooner is better than later!

Don't make the mistake the Israelites made, in thinking he would come a warrior king, as some said;
instead, he was born of a woman; Mary wrapped Him in swaddling clothes and laid Him in a manger bed. Luke 2:7

John bore witness about Him, "This was He of whom I said, "He who comes after me ranks before me," Matthew 3:11
Scripture tells us; And from His fullness we have all received, grace upon grace, through faith we see. John 1:17

You Lord, laid the foundations of the earth in the beginning, and the heavens are the work of your hands,
they will perish, they will all wear out like a garment, but you and your children will always stand.

The creator of heaven and earth suffered and bled and died for His creation, then rose again, so we live and move and have our being with elation!

That makes Christmas a blessed surprise; the uncreated, eternal, and infinite God comes right here among us as our light and life.

So we can meet each day in this sinful world, grow in our faith and walk as a Christian through battles already won with His strife!

In Christ's Service,
Composed by the Holy Spirit and written by Reverend Paul E. Yanke
For Christmas Day Service

Feast In The Way

God sent prophets, priests, and kings through the years to people both good and bad,
all because God loved His creations and free eternal life for them He had.

God's representatives the people did hurt, torture, and some even they did kill,
so God through His gracious love sent His only Son to save, because it was His will.

If you can't see God's hand in nature all around us, then open up your eyes,
and through the Holy Spirit, you will realize, "it happened by chance" is just a pack of lies.

When I see God send a rainbow by day, and vast stars in the sky at night,
I know He has always kept His promises and leads those in faith by the light!

Each time we open our eyes to face the challenges of another day,
we know God has touched us and gives power to walk in the Way!

God preserved His history, that we may see Christ as the Living Word,
He gave the Lord's Supper, a taste of Heaven that the Gospel message be heard!

There are many kinds of feasts to enjoy on this old earth,
but without the gift of heaven, nothing is what their worth.

There is a veritable feast for the eyes in Fall that I see,
and when I think of the care God took in creating it for you and me,
I realize how wonderful the feast in heaven must be!

Based on: Matthew 22: 1 - 14

Composed by the Holy Spirit and written by Reverend Paul E. Yanke

For My Ailing Mom

Life is what you make of it; this is most certainly true,
but when you are a child of God, everyday is fresh and new.

Because of original sin life sometimes deals out pain we would rather not
endure,
since God's love and provision are always with us we remain steadfast and
secure.

Once you kept up a daily routine nurturing and feeding baby me that I
might grow into a man,
now I return the favor, feeding and nurturing you, so physically you regain
strength for God's plan.

There is no way to understand in this world what love really is,
unless you have a personal relationship with Jesus Christ and in His
example do persist.

Scripture states life is meaningless utterly meaningless to people who don't
have a care,
Christians know life isn't meaningless as the Holy Spirit lives in them so
the devil beware.

To occupy my time as a child you had me sewing buttons on a card,
it taught me how to mend my clothes and bear up in faith when times are
hard.

You read to me when I was small to help me learn my A, B, C's,
now I read to you as you recover your long hours to appease.

You taught us the value of property by not giving us everything for which
we asked,
that we must work hard and reach for the stars, to obtain things that will
last.

The value of faith in God you drove home to us by making sure we always
attended Sunday School and Church,
we never questioned why we just got ready without a word, to question our
parents would have meant for us the worst.

You fixed our owies and boo-boos with the love of Christ and respect,
I can't fix your injury with a kiss, but know God will not you neglect.

Growing up under your mentoring and care, truly was the best,
you taught us hard work, responsibility and leave to God all the rest.

With you and dad we learned not just by instruction, but most importantly
by example,
how to be loving, carrying and compassionate of others and not on their
rights trample.

We thank God He gave us you as are parent and not another,
for us it's just not acceptable for another, that we could call her Mother.

Mom we pray with all our hearts and God heals you making you well,
thanks for all the positive memories that make our hearts and minds swell.
And for always making us ready others of our faith to tell.

Composed by the Holy Spirit and written by Reverend Paul E. Yanke

God's Biblical Love

One thing I've observed is that worldly love is shallow and only skin deep,
that's why many are visibly smitten and jump into marriage with a speedy
leap.

As a Christian Cop I was sent to keep the peace at many a domestic dispute,
where a husband beat his wife as though she were a piece of property or loot.

I would stand there looking at the wife bleeding, as she told me he loves
me, after all he's my spouse,
woman you don't understand what love is, if he loved you he wouldn't beat
you, he's a sinner acting like a louse.

Love is so much more than just a word that you say,
it's a caring that's shown by following God's Way.

The Bible states; if I speak in the tongues of angels, but have not love I am
only a resounding gong,
so when I try to show love from a worldly standpoint, I fail my presentation
is in reality all wrong.

Our God is loving, but also just and vengeful this is absolutely true,
He wishes all men to be saved from the fire of hell, shouldn't we too?

In this world imperfection, sin in love is the best we can hope for,
ah, but in heaven love is perfect, keeps no record of wrongs, is so much more.

Jesus replied; "All the commandments in God's Word, the Law can be summed up in just two,"
love the Lord God with all your heart, soul, and mind, and love your neighbor as much as you. Matthew 22:37-40

When I was a child, I talked, thought and reasoned like a child,
as a man I put evil ways behind me, my temperament is mild. 1 Corinthians 13:11

I've come to the conclusion, it's impossible to love as God desires without realizing that Christ died for our sins on the cross,
we can be a good neighbor, try to help those in need, but without Christ our Savior all is poor human dross.

Love is patient; love is kind, does not envy or boast, and is never ever proud,
Jesus lived these attributes, and with the Holy Ghost, if were listening we hear then out loud
1 Corinthians 13:1-13

God knows us fully, we see a poor reflection as in a mirror, and know only in part,
in Heaven we shall fully know, God's perfection because Jesus see's into all of the human heart.

We love because He first loved us, shed His blood, and rose from the dead; to believe is a must,
so follow Christ's example of love to our fellow man, and remember all our feeble attempts are but lust.

Jesus Christ has given us this very strong standing command,
whoever loves God must also love his brother, this I demand! Matthew 6:14-15

1 Corinthians 13, 1 John 4:7-21, Matthew 22:37-40

Composed by the Holy Spirit and written by Reverend Paul E. Yanke

God's Law and Gospel

In these times that are hard to endure,
of many decisions and things I'm unsure.

It seems the harder and harder I work,
the more my time spent seems like a quirk.

Many thoughts weight heavy on my mind,
and that's when you appreciate someone being kind.

We were all put on God's green earth for a reason,
although many times our road is rocky and unpleasin'.

Keep your eye on the far horizon they'll say,
But oh Lord that's when I'm glad I can pray.

A man needs time to relax and reflect on his past,
and say to himself I haven't given out my last.

I am a man who knows God has given him friends, who are dear,
for a person without Christian friends is in trouble, I fear.

The law of God the Father is good, just, and wise,
and without it's guidance we are open to the world's lies.

Jesus said: Nothing that enters a man from outside can make him unclean,
it is from within, out of the men's hearts evil thoughts make men mean.
Matthew 15:11

Do not add to the law I give you and do not subtract,
for to do such a thing, God's commands lose their impact. Revelation
22:18-19

Lord through the mirror of your law you show me I'm a sinner,
in the Holy Spirit forgiveness and eternal life you make me a winner.

God your law has caused me to walk many a mile,
for to have faith in your Gospel make my heart smile.

I cherish the time I spend in word and prayer with you,
and by the Holy Spirit I give you my heart in trusting you do too.

Composed by the Holy Spirit and written by Reverend Paul E. Yanke

Good Friday - Jesus Suffered For Me

When I think of Jesus suffering and try to comprehend His pain,
as I contemplate on His misery the meaning becomes quite plain. Psalm 22

I don't deserve such a loving Savior; a sacrificial Lamb was He,
Jesus followed His Father's will, died for such a miserable sinner as me.
John 1:29

Innocent yet scourged for our transgressions, to try and satisfy the Jews,
we should think long and hard on this, as we sit comfortably in our pews.
Luke 22:63-65

False accusations made against Him, liars came forward willingly false
testimony to give,
the Pharisees patience was wearing thin; they knew this Jesus of Nazareth
couldn't be allowed to live. Matthew 26:59

Finally two came forward "destroy the temple and in three days I'll rebuild
it", that is what He said, Matthew 26:60-61
the high priest asked Jesus "tell us if you are the Christ," the Sanhedrin now
were by the devil led. Matthew 26:63

"Yes, it is as you say" Jesus finally replied, Matthew 26:64
the high priest said He's guilty it can not be denied.

In the future you will see the Son of Man,
at the right hand of the mighty one the great I AM.

Look said the high priest no more witnesses are needed, He is guilty of blasphemy,
then they spit in His face and struck Him with fists, asking who might it be?

Jesus predicted Peter would deny Him, no Master you I love and will never leave,
but before the rooster crowed, three times Peter lied, Jesus enemies to deceive.

Now off to Pilate He was taken because the Sanhedrin could not impose the death penalty,
Pilate found out Jesus was a Galilean and sent Him to Herod who expected a show adding more mockery.

Herod was mad when for him Jesus would not perform,
so back to Pilate he was sent to suffer much more scorn.

Pilate offered up Barabbas in hope that the people would buy it,
but sentenced Jesus to death because he was afraid of a riot.

Off to the place of the Skull Jesus was led,
because the Pharisees couldn't wait to see Him dead.

Nailed to a cross innocently was our Savior, Messiah, Redeemer, friend,
but contrary to popular belief when Jesus said; "it is finished" it was not the end. John 19:30

In front of His accusers with two thieves and His mother to see,
Jesus died as the thief and Centurion attest to set all believers free.

Make no mistake about it; the Jews weren't the only ones to nail Jesus to that tree,
Good Friday reminds us; because we are sinful we are guilty as well, both you and me!

Biblical References; Matthew 26:57 – 27:56 & Luke 22:54 – 23:43

Composed by the Holy Spirit and written by Reverend Paul E. Yanke

If Wishes Were Reality, A Merry Christmas I'd Have

If I could stop all the politicians from lying, cheating and stealing,
and get them to turn to Christ Jesus for His holy healing.

If only people would remember the Second Greatest Commandment and
be fair in all their business dealings, (Matt. 22)
then I as a person, a Christian could foster greater respect for my fellow
man in my feelings.

Were countries to stop fighting, killing, and all wars to cease and desist?
(Psalm 46)
then I could think about something festive and simple, like a peppermint
twist.

When you watch the news or read the newspaper the articles are mostly
downers and all bad,
if only reporters could recognize the importance of acknowledging the
good, my heart would be glad.

It seems to us as Christians that mankind couldn't go more astray,
if only they would repent, look to the Lord and earnestly pray. (1 John 3:8-10)

Society has taught many of our children to be rude, self-centered, and vain, and opened the door for the devil to pour evil down, like drops of rain.

Young parents need to recognize again the importance of teaching their children God's Word,
so that they will be protected from the devil and into his evil not be lured.
(Eph. 6:10-18)

Adults a false teaching they have been taught as though it were truth, (John 14:6)
that even Christians are to be accepting of what anyone believes is so couth.

God blesses from Christmas to Christmas, three hundred and sixty five days when I wake and see light,
for without Christ in one's life all is despair, suffering, death, darkness, and black as night.
(Matt. 5:14, Luke 2:32, John 1)

Oh, all these negatives if I were not a Christian I would count to be loss,
Except that I know for my sins Jesus in my place went to the cross. Matthew, Mark, Luke & John

Born in a stable, grew up a carpenter and raised from the dead to set us free,
Jesus part of the Triune God is my Savior, comforter, deliver, and Lord for you must see. Matthew, Mark, Luke & John

A Merry Christmas I will have, my joy it won't affect, (Rev. 20:11-15, John 3:16)
for I know God is in control, for all His chosen elect!

Composed by the Holy Spirit and written by Reverend Paul E. Yanke

Little Church
On The Hill

The little church on the hill today is so still,
we know the Holy Spirit is present everywhere by God's Will.

This house of God, was built to stay,
as a place for its members, to worship and pray.

Little children in Sunday school, as the teacher fights the time on the clock,
as Bible stories of the Shepherd Jesus, make them part of the flock.

At one time with members, this church did swell,
to preach and teach, the Gospel story to tell.

Church denominations are not what matters here,
because all true Christians must shed a tear.

Church members should know, their work was not in vein,
because to many a Christian the Gospel was made plain.

Although from these walls the congregation now parts,
the Lord's mysterious ways may still soften hearts.

It's important to remember, the congregation never ceases to exist,
where faith in their Savior, the Lord Jesus persists.

Composed by the Holy Spirit and written by Reverend Paul E. Yanke

On Faith

There is a God, all nature cries. The air I breathe 'tis His, is no lie.
I see it painted on the skies, I see it in the flowering spring, I hear it when the birds sing.

There is a God, all nature cries, I see it in the flowing mains.
I feel it when I plow the plains, plant the seeds, and anticipate His rains. I see it in His fruitful plans.

There is a God, all nature cries, I see it on the fruitful terrain.
I see it stamped on hail and snow; I see it where the streams flow. I feel it when all comes together, and I know not how!

There is a God, all nature cries, I see it in the clouds that roam.
I hear it when the thunders roar, that for us life may never be a boar by the power of the Holy Spirit take the free life given that we may soar!

There is a God, all nature cries, I see it when the morning shines.
Another day, a gift, life to refine, I even see it when the day declines. In restful sleep, so tomorrow I thank the Devine!

There is a God, all nature cries, I see it in the mountain height.
I see it in the smallest mite, When the Lord's Prayer I recite. I feel—I know, there is a God!

There is a God, all nature cries, How could I look and believe otherwise. Sinful man doesn't understand the simplest workings of his body. Faith picks us up, when faulty human reason is shoddy.

God speaks to me; I know 'tis true,
because the Triune God provides all to be made anew!

Composed by the Holy Spirit and written by Reverend Paul E. Yanke

Season's Of Faith

A man was born to German parents on All Hollow's Eve, in the year nineteen thirty one,
soon after his parents had him baptized Lutheran, his salvation to be won.

His family like all was not perfect, of this he truly knew,
but they took him to Sunday School, and his faith really grew.

Confirmation class when he was a teenager, he took to with great energy and zeal,
even if it meant walking three miles to church, it didn't matter it made God's Word real.

He learned the Ten Commandments and took them to heart,
confession of sins, forgiveness, at least it was a start.

Slightly crippled hands he had all of his natural life,
but because of his Faith no problem just a little strife.

He became a farmer and soldier in spite of his size,
and with determination and ingenuity to the occasion did rise.

Tilling and planting by toil his crops, with the tools of the trade,
he felt close to God, for dust you are, and from dust you were made.

He did much in the surrounding area to develop goodwill,
through his writing, thankfulness in his fellow humans, he did instill.

Although he was old school, and a little rough around the edges,
as a missionary for his church, he to the Lord his heart pledges.

Serving as Elder and Confirmation teacher that the youth may learn,
become strong in their Faith and in trials to Jesus turn!

This man knew he was both Saint and a terrible sinner,
and because of this knowledge it made him a winner.

Justification by Grace through faith in Jesus, your sins God forgives,
and now throughout all eternity in Heaven's Bliss this man lives.

Composed by the Holy Spirit and written by Reverend Paul E. Yanke

Thanksgiving Means Thanksliving

It occurred to me to be in a constant mindset of worship and Thanksgiving,
I must live my life as a constant example of Christ's life, Thanksliving.
(John 6:38-40)

To be thankful for even the trials and thorns in life I must face,
because Christ knows through such education I will persevere and win
life's race. (Acts 20:24)

God sent Moses and Aaron to Pharaoh of Egypt and ordered him to let
My people go,
but as part of God's plan, through hardening of the heart all Pharaoh could
say was NO.
(Exodus)

Moses continued to pray and follow God's instructions to the tee,
Pharaoh finally said, go, get out of here, please and be free. (Exodus)

God's people should have been thankful worshipping God, filled with joy;
instead they complained and wined against Moses their faith to destroy.
(Exodus)

King David, God's second anointed leader of His people lived a life of sin, distress, and pain,
and in Psalms we read of David's true repentance, God's forgiveness, honor, blessings on him did rain. (2 Samuel)

If ever a prophet lived who from a human standpoint we would say his life was not one for thanksgiving,
Queen Jezebel wanted to kill him, yet trusting in God, live Elijah went to heaven because he lived a life of Thanksliving. (1 Kings 17 – 2 Kings 2)

Just think of Queen Esther who trusted the Holy Spirit to soften the Persian King Xerxes heart, that to save her people's lives, God's Israelites, she must take a chance strengthened faith to impart. (Esther)

What a day of rejoicing was heard all throughout the Persian land,
they were able to defend themselves against their enemies through God's intervening hand. (Esther)

Being truly thankful is about realizing God's divine providence in my life, and without it everything I do is filled with meaningless pain and strife. (Ecclesiastes 2:18-26)

A man once said; "I don't need to thank God" because I live and eat by the sweat of my brow, what a fool this man is because God could take his life and I mean here and now. (Proverbs 9:10-12)

To me I must recognize each seed that sprouts and grows;
my food and drink are from God surely He knows. (Isaiah 55:10)

The air I breathe and a place to lay my head are only a loan,
and as a child of God, my heart and soul are His, me He does own. (John 1:12)

Your human sinful sacrifices are not acceptable to God, that's not true Thanksgiving,
A broken and contrite heart is what God desires, His Will always, that's faithful Thanksliving!

Composed by the Holy Spirit and written by Reverend Paul E. Yanke

The Garden

To me a garden is a wonderful place, more than just a thing,
I head off to it with pleasure, and to it my thoughts bring.

For me it's a place of healthy exercise and of solitude,
never a place of wandering thoughts to this world rude.

I love to plant the little seeds, in the warm earth upon my knees.
Pray for rain so the seeds will sprout, it still amazes me when plants pop out.

The garden reminds me of Jesus parable of the mustard seed, though it is
the smallest of all it grows into the largest of plants, actually a tree,
the seed represents faith sown by a believer, watered, and nurtured by the
Holy Spirit it grows so the blind can be healed, and the truth see. Matthew
13, Mark 4, Luke 13

What an awesome God we have to have created the circle of life in such a way,
that with a little care and work it will provide our every need, day by day.

When working in the garden I think of Genesis 3:19, when God stated "Now
you will work by the sweet of your brow,"
become planters of seed for the Holy Spirit and God will work the miracle
of faith, the when and how.

We must not be sluggards as it warns in the book of Proverbs,
there is no room for laziness or our bellies situation will be adverse.

We must not just plant the seeds and leave them to fend for themselves all along the way,
or it will be Like Jesus Parable of the Sower, most plants won't make it to see another day.
Matthew 13, Mark 4, Luke 8

When I dig in the dirt and look up at a tree, I see the cross, Jesus dying in our place to make us free.
I think of Jesus who being God's only Son could have chosen any place to pray, but He chose the Garden of Gethsemane,

He prayed, "Father if it be possible lift this cup from me,"
but He knew He must die and rise for you and me!
Matthew 26, Mark 14, Luke 22

Just as all seeds must die to bring forth new life,
Jesus died and rose delivering believers from eternal strife!
Matthew 27,28 Mark 15, 16 Luke 23, 24 John 19, 20

Composed by the Holy Spirit and written by Reverend Paul E. Yanke
(This poem may be used for Maunday Thursday)

The True Christmas Story

So that we may understand in due time,
I give to you the story of God's love in rhyme.

God sent prophets, priests, and kings through the years to people both good and bad,
all because God loved His creations and free eternal life for them He had.

The first prophesy of Jesus coming was recorded in Genesis some four thousand years before He arrived,
Moses recorded in 3:15, "He will crush your head, and you will strike His heel" that mankind may be revived.

Some fourteen hundred years before His birth,
prophets foretold of a Savior that would come to earth.

Isaiah foretold 700 years before the royal baby's birth,
a virgin will be with child, and Christ come to earth. (Isaiah 9:6-7)

In the sixth month God sent the angel Gabriel to Nazareth a town in Galilee,
told the Virgin Mary, to you a child will be born, of the Holy Spirit to set people free. (Luke 1:26-35)

Bethlehem is the town where Jesus was to be born,
and even though predicted by prophets, some would scorn. (Micah 5:2)

He was to be born in a stable manger, because no room at the inn,
born of Virgin Mary to save the world from sin. (Isaiah 7:14)

Caesar Augustus issued a decree that a census should occur,
and all, everyone went to his hometown to register.

Joseph went up from Nazareth to Bethlehem to register with Mary his pledged wife,
while there it came time to deliver Jesus, His people to save from strife.

She wrapped Him in swaddling clothes and placed Him in a manger,
because there was no room for them in the inn as strangers. (Luke 2:1-7)

Shepherds were abiding in the fields nearby,
when an angel of the Lord appeared in the sky.

Do not be afraid the angel did say,
a Savior is born in Bethlehem today. (Luke 2:8-12)

A company of heavenly host appeared praising God and saying,
Glory to God in the highest, on earth peace is staying. (Luke 2:13-14)

The shepherds went to see this miracle and with their eyes behold,
they returned glorifying and praising God for the message to all they told (Luke 2:16-18)

Men during the time of the Messiah's birth in their own sins did whorl,
because they were looking for a warrior king they missed baby Jesus as their pearl. (Jeremiah & Zephaniah)

Although this true story occurred over two thousand years in the past,
the salvation it brought continues to last and last!

Contrary to popular tradition the Magi didn't visit Jesus in the stable on His birth night, but rather as Matthew makes clear visited months later the house, following God's glorious star light.

We don't even know the number of Magi, but assume from gifts of gold, Incense, and myrrh, there were three,
its true these wise men came from the east, bearing gifts to worship, but many more in number could be!

But having been warned in a dream not to tell King Herod what they had learned all about,
after opening their gifts and presenting then to Jesus they returned to their country by another route.

After the wise men left, an angel of the Lord appeared to Joseph in a dream, escape to the land of Egypt with the baby Jesus to foil King Herod's deathly scheme. Matthew 2, fulfillment of Hosea 11:1)

Let us recognize God's love in Jesus birth that with us it may be well, then will the Holy spirit through us shine so the number of believers swell!

Our little country church on the mountain is all aglow,
the light of God's love, stain-glassed patterns reflect on the snow.

This message of Jesus Christ our Savior, who died on the cross, must not be kept in these walls or to the world it is loss.

The Gospel of the Christmas message we will, we must share, that the world in darkness for Christ's second coming can prepare.

God's plan is so perfect and great in sending His Son
that those who are moved to faith may be won. (Luke 21:28)

To pave the way for the awaited Savior's coming,
God sent a messenger to bring human minds to strumming. (Luke 1:13, 3:1-6)

Repent and be baptized John the Baptist did say,
God's Word refines and prepares you for the narrow way. (Luke 3:7-18)

Composed by the Holy Spirit and written by Reverend Paul E. Yanke

To A Pastor's Wife

I can't imagine life without you,
it would be empty and blue.

We are a match made in heaven,
I know God will bless us seven times eleven.

You lift me up when I'm down,
and won't let me make myself the clown.

You're encouragement is just what I need to perform at my best,
and you help me to remember to God leave the rest.

God knew what a great team we would truly make,
and how frustrated it would make the devil for the Lord's sake.

So let's buck up in the ministry, when the going gets tough,
and realize that God's Word says the Holy Spirit's enough.

We as sinful human beings are too weak, God's sheep to lead,
but Scripture tells us our weakness is God's strength, we will succeed.
2 Corinthians 12:9

Composed by the Holy Spirit and written by Reverend Paul E. Yanke

Tractor Puller's Prayer

A prayer of safety for all who compete,
That our joy in our hobby may be complete.

So go to your tractors and fire them up boys,
Time to have some fun with your big boy toys.

Not wanting to slight the girls who intend,
To give the boys a hard time as they contend.

What a colorful group of rednecks who fan the pulling flame,
How boring life would be if God had made us all the same.

Some of us grew up on a farm as our back-ground,
One things for sure among the rest the country minded abound.

Some of us prefer the Putt Putt of an old John Deere,
For pulling on dead weight nothing can match a two lugger.

Others prefer the purr of a tractor in the color of red,
You see a Farmall is what they dream of while in bed.

The choice of some pullers is a yellow Minnie Moline,
For pulling on a weight machine they can be keen.

Ribbons and trophies won, we place on a shelf,
But friendships last, and are more important to self.

It is important how you live and play the game,
Winning when you've done the work yourself is true fame.

Sooner or later by the Holy Spirit with an open mind,
We realize all we have is because God is so kind.

Things of this world may be nice and flatter,
But faith in Jesus Christ is truly what matters!

Composed by the Holy Spirit and written by Reverend Paul E. Yanke

T'was The Night Before Christmas

T'was the night before Christmas, when all through God's House,
not a creature was stirring, not even a church mouse.

The candles on the altar are lighted with care,
in anticipation for baby Jesus, who soon would be there.

The choir has carefully practiced songs and they are ablaze,
perfectly executed voices to Christ we sing praise.

Our children have apprehensively worked on their parts,
and will help tell the story to touch human hearts.

The Christmas Tree was decorated with lights and loving hands,
the Angels remind us that for each of us God has plans.

The candles on the Advent Wreath are all glowing,
the end of the Advent Season are showing.

Those who don't have faith are warned to beware,
because this is the season for Jesus to prepare. 1 Thessalonians 5:2

The Messiah a descendent of King David would be,
in this the Old Testament people salvation could see. Isaiah 7:13-14

In Micah he tells chapter five, verse two,
the Savior in Bethlehem comes to you.

The Lord himself shall give you a sign, behold a virgin shall conceive,
by the power of the Holy Spirit bear a son that you believe. Isaiah 7:14

For to us a child is born, to us a Son is given, Isaiah 9:6
thirty-three years later through His sacrifice, we're forgiven.

John the Baptist was the person, who prepared the way,
John preached in the wilderness the Bible does say. Matthew 3

When Mary greeted her cousin the babe John leaped in Elizabeth's womb,
the good news Mary brought proved the Holy Spirit's power to save ALL
from doom.
Luke 1:39-45

A lot of time passes after Malachi the Jewish people tells a Savior is coming,
four-hundred years before John preached in the wilderness I'm summing.

Matthew shows us Jesus the King of all kings,
and because of this info our hearts do sing.

Mark shows us Jesus the Servant, who frees,
Heaven the faith of children belongs to these.

Luke shows us that Jesus is the Son of man,
a carpenter living among us as part of God's plan.

John shows us that Jesus is Son of God and Shepherd of the sheep,
and as His chosen Lambs in safety and faith He does now keep.

Caesar Augustus issued a decree that a census should occur,
and all, everyone went to his hometown to register.

Joseph went up from Nazareth to Bethlehem to register with Mary his pledged wife,
while there it came time to deliver Jesus His people to save from strife.
Luke 2:1-6

She wrapped Him in swaddling clothes and placed Him in a manger,
because there was no room for them in the inn as strangers. Luke 2:7

Shepherds were abiding in the fields nearby,
when an Angel of the Lord appeared in the sky. Luke 2:8-18

Do not be afraid the Angel did say,
a Savior is born in Bethlehem today. Luke 2:10-12

A company of heavenly host appeared praising God and saying,
glory to God in the highest, on earth peace is staying. Luke 2:13-14

The shepherds went to see this miracle and with their eyes behold,
they returned glorifying and praising God for the message to all they told.
Luke 2:16-18

Although this true story occurred over two-thousand years in the past,
the salvation it brought continues to last and last.

Our little country church on the mountain is all aglow,
the light of God's love, stain-glassed patterns reflect on the snow.

This message of Jesus Christ our Savior, who died on the cross,
must not be kept in these walls or to the world it is loss. Luke 10:2

The Gospel of the Christmas message we must share,
that the world in darkness for Christ's Second Coming can prepare.

Merry CHRISTmas in the Gospel Light,
And to all believers a good night!

Scripture References: Matthew, Mark, Luke, John, specifically Matt. 2, 27,28, 28:18-20,

Mark 1,14-16, Luke 1,2,3,20,23,24, John 1,5,10,19,20, Micah 5:2, Isaiah 7:13-14, 9:6,
Acts 1,2, Romans 5-8, Genesis 3:15 and elsewhere throughout the Bible.

Composed by the Holy Spirit and written by Reverend Paul E. Yanke

Verses for a Pastor's Wife's Birthday

Being a faithful Pastor in an alien world is extremely hard today,
Especially when with the help of the devil you let sin get in the way.

There was a time when I was all but ready to quit,
because the devil was making me feel really quite unfit.

I knew I needed someone as a partner, with faith as strong as mine,
someone to work not against me, but with me in God's good time.

The thought of dating was really, really scary,
but in prayer I found one, she's just berries.

I had ideas of what I was looking for it is actually true,
and God's Will gives what's best and for me that's you.

It was ordained by God that we should over the phone, fall in love, and then meet,
because of this our love is based on faith which is strongest, you've made our family complete.

You're love for the Lord is evident in all you say and do,
all people around you are blessed because they know you are true.

Thank goodness God doesn't give us what we deserve, but what we really need,
That our faith may be nurtured, strengthened on the right track with His seed.

Well Happy _____ Birthday Babe, you've helped keep my faith strong and alive,
and by the way I really don't think you look a day over thirty-five.

Maybe it's because I'm bald and don't have any hair,
that everyone who does looks younger, as over their head they don't have air.

You light up a room for us all especially me,
May God make it so forever and into eternity!

Composed by the Holy Spirit and written by Reverend Paul E. Yanke

Worry/Anxiety

Self-inflicted pain is so evil; it robs me of my joy,
when I allow the devil, with my thoughts to toy.

Darkness closes in all around me; I concentrate on every minute of pain,
despair and desperation attack me, on all my thoughts it does nothing but
rain.

Anxiety convinces you it's over, your physical life, your body it will kill,
I'm living proof that's not true, for forty years I've lived with it, and I'm
here still.

Doom and gloom are so defeating the feeling I just hate,
Jesus is light, and reminds me He holds my eternal fate.

The more I try to fight it, the worse it really seems to get,
humanly it's just not possible, too win God's power is the only sure bet.

By trusting in Jesus the Lord will drive the devil away,
and pondering on God's Word, the Holy Spirit will keep him at bay.

Constructive thinking and mental distraction will help to keep your mind
in line,
practice no stink in think in; concentrate on God's promises and you'll be
just fine.

Desperation sets in; your thoughts and life seem to come to a stall
but through experience as a Christian; Christ can help you stand again tall.

Be careful of your hearts, or with anxieties they will be weighed down,
instead keep your heart on Jesus, or the devil will make you the clown.
Luke 21:34

Who of you by worrying can add a single day to his life?
Your Heavenly Father loves you; let Him handle your strife. Matthew
6:26,27.

Do not worry about what you will eat, drink, or wear,
for I am Jesus your Lord and I do for you care. Matthew 6:25

In everything by prayer, with thanksgiving to God present your requests,
and God will give you His peace, guard your heart, do for you what's best.
Philippians 4:6

Cast all your anxiety on the Lord and He will care for you,
know that He is the Great Physician; believe for you it's true. 1 Peter 5:7

Composed by the Holy Spirit and written by Reverend Paul E. Yanke

Ye Olde Cross

Christ said the church is the people,
it's not about the building or steeple.

Christ's sacrifice to save all of man-kind,
when you look at this cross, should you remind.

Christ the God-man shed His blood on the cross that we might see;
He paid the price for our sins and iniquities to set us all free.

He rose on the third day, and provided for us the way.

This cross a crucifix is not, it is empty, and on its own does stand,
it affirms that the Savior I trust now sits at God's right hand.

Just as God created and blessed the growing of the wood from which this
cross was cut,
He is the author and perfecter of our faith that we aren't left in an endless rut.

This beautifully preserved cross, yet singed with fire,
shows faith is strengthened by trial, God's true desire.

If the walls of this sanctuary of the great I AM could talk,
they would tell of God's people and their stumbling, but faithful walk.

This piece of a firm foundation that has stood the test of time, represents God's claim; hell shall not prevail against this church of mine.

Composed by the Holy Spirit and written by Reverend Paul E. Yanke.

Printed in the United States
By Bookmasters